For Cecelia,
Reading is a hoot!
Katy Jo

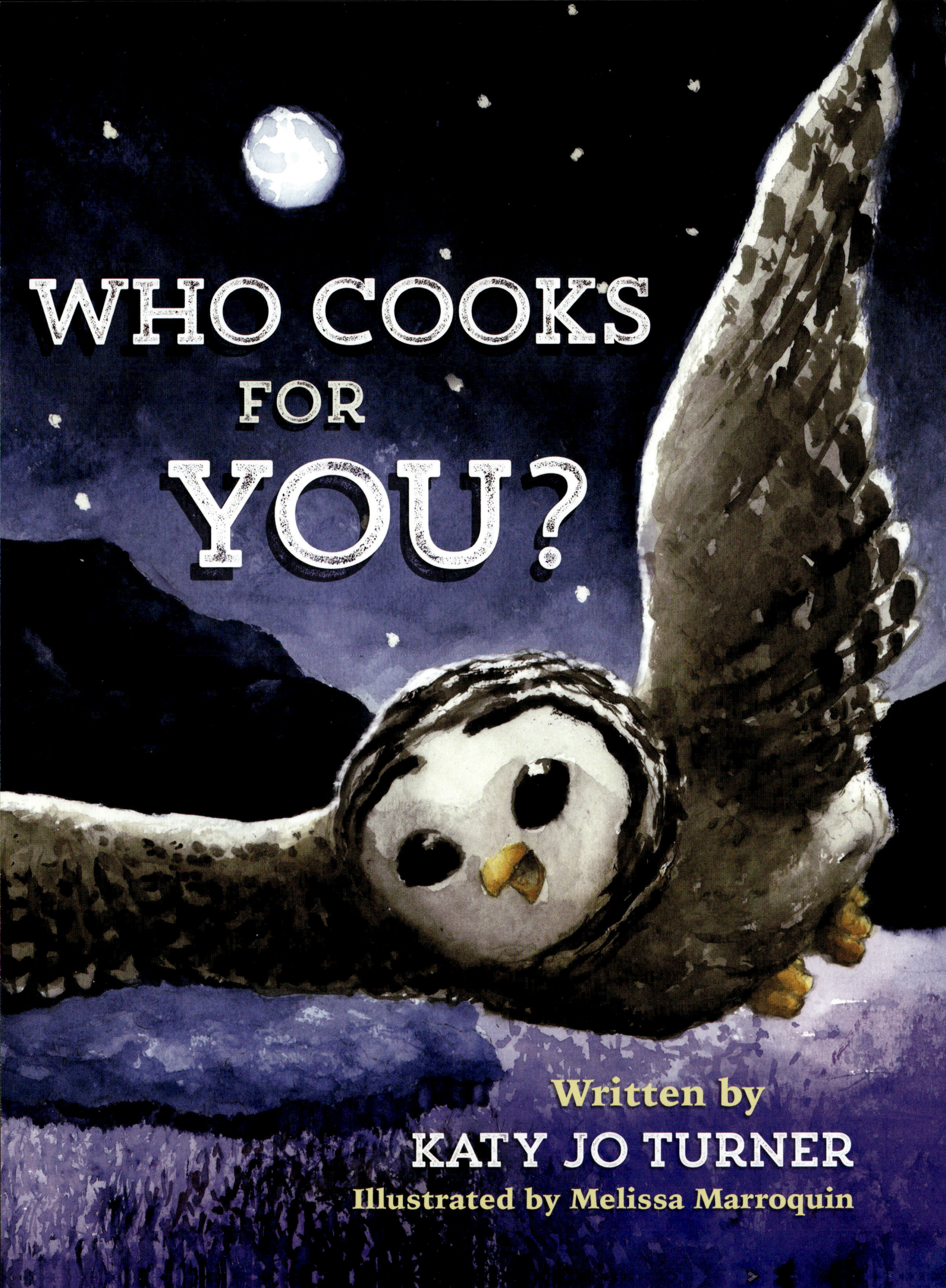
WHO COOKS
FOR
YOU?
Written by
KATY JO TURNER
Illustrated by Melissa Marroquin

Edited by Angela Wiechmann
Illustrated by Melissa Marroquin

ISBN 13: 978-1-59298-668-2
Library of Congress Catalog Number: 2015918421
Printed in the United States of America
First Printing: 2015
19 18 17 16 15 5 4 3 2 1

Cover and interior design by Dan Pitts
Author headshot by Laine Torres Photography

Beaver's Pond Press, Inc.
7108 Ohms Lane
Edina, MN 55439–2129
www.BeaversPondPress.com

To order, visit www.KatyJoTurner.com.
Reseller discounts available.

A special thanks to the Whistle Stop Cafe, Frontenac, MN, for allowing this book to celebrate the delightful diner.

KATY JO TURNER comes up with her best story ideas when out in the woods. She knows a bit about owls from her days as an environmental educator, and she knows a lot about being hungry. This is her first children's book.

MELISSA MARROQUIN began her career as an illustrator at the age of six when she drew all over the back of the family sofa. She has a BFA in illustration and specializes in children's books.

To my HBs

WHO COOKS FOR YOUUU?

is what Howie the barred owl says.

It can mean . . . "How are you?"

or "Wow, that moon is big!"

or "Those frogs are *noisy*!"

But today his call meant something different.

This morning, before even the sun was up in the sky, Howie was hungry. He *always* ate his breakfast before it was light out, and he *always* got his own food. But today Howie was feeling lazy.

Today he wanted someone to make *him* breakfast. This morning his

WHO COOKS FOR YOUUU?

really meant: "Who cooks for *you*?"

Whom could he ask?

He flew up to a doe quietly wandering by.

He yelled,

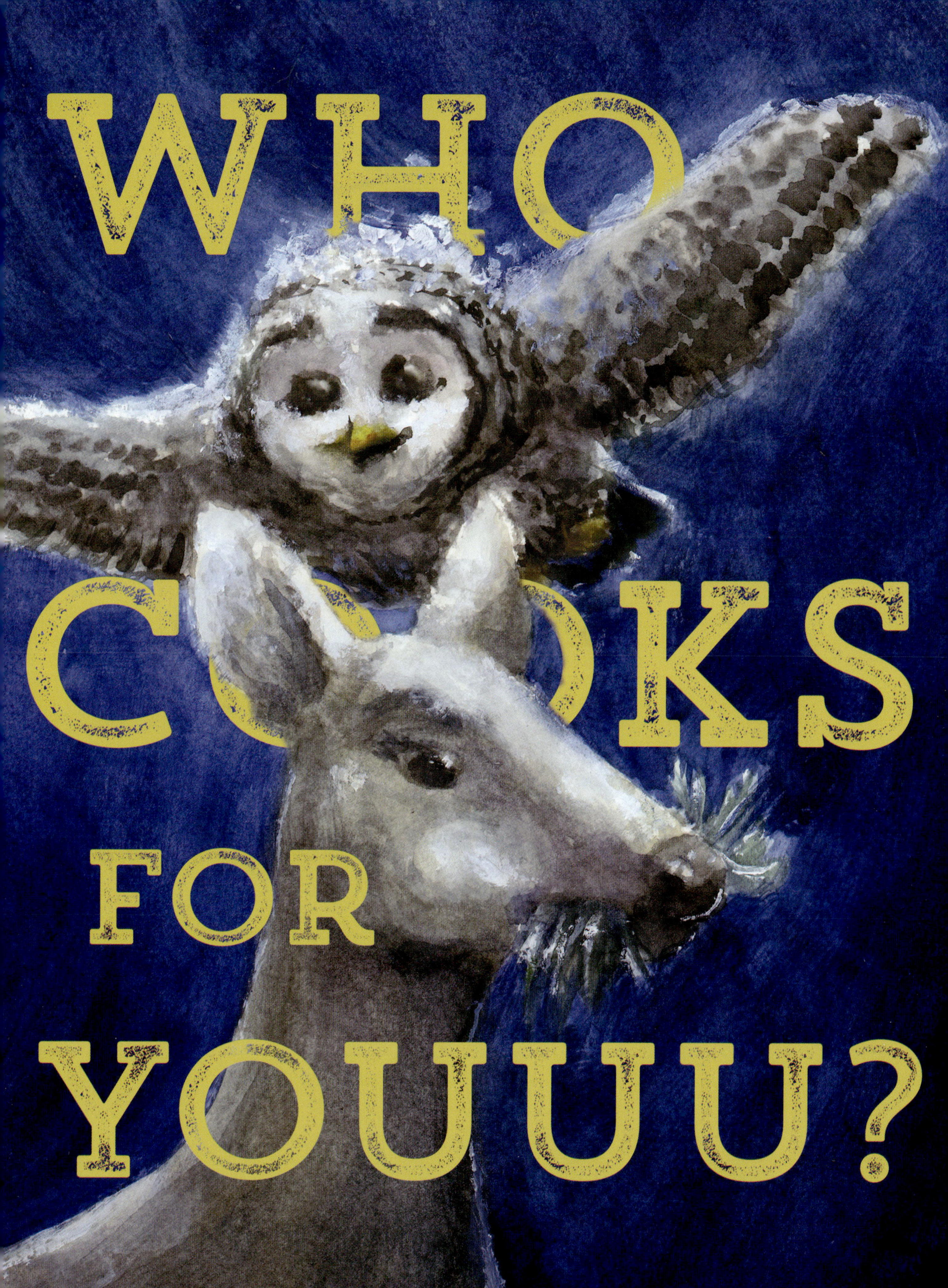
WHO
COOKS
FOR
YOUUU?

But it didn't go so well.

Instead of answering,
she gave a stomp that meant
"Too loud!"

STOMP!

"Too close!"

STOMP!

"Too early!"

STOMP!

And then she ran away.

Though still hungry, Howie wasn't worried.
There had to be other animals awake this early
who would help him find breakfast.

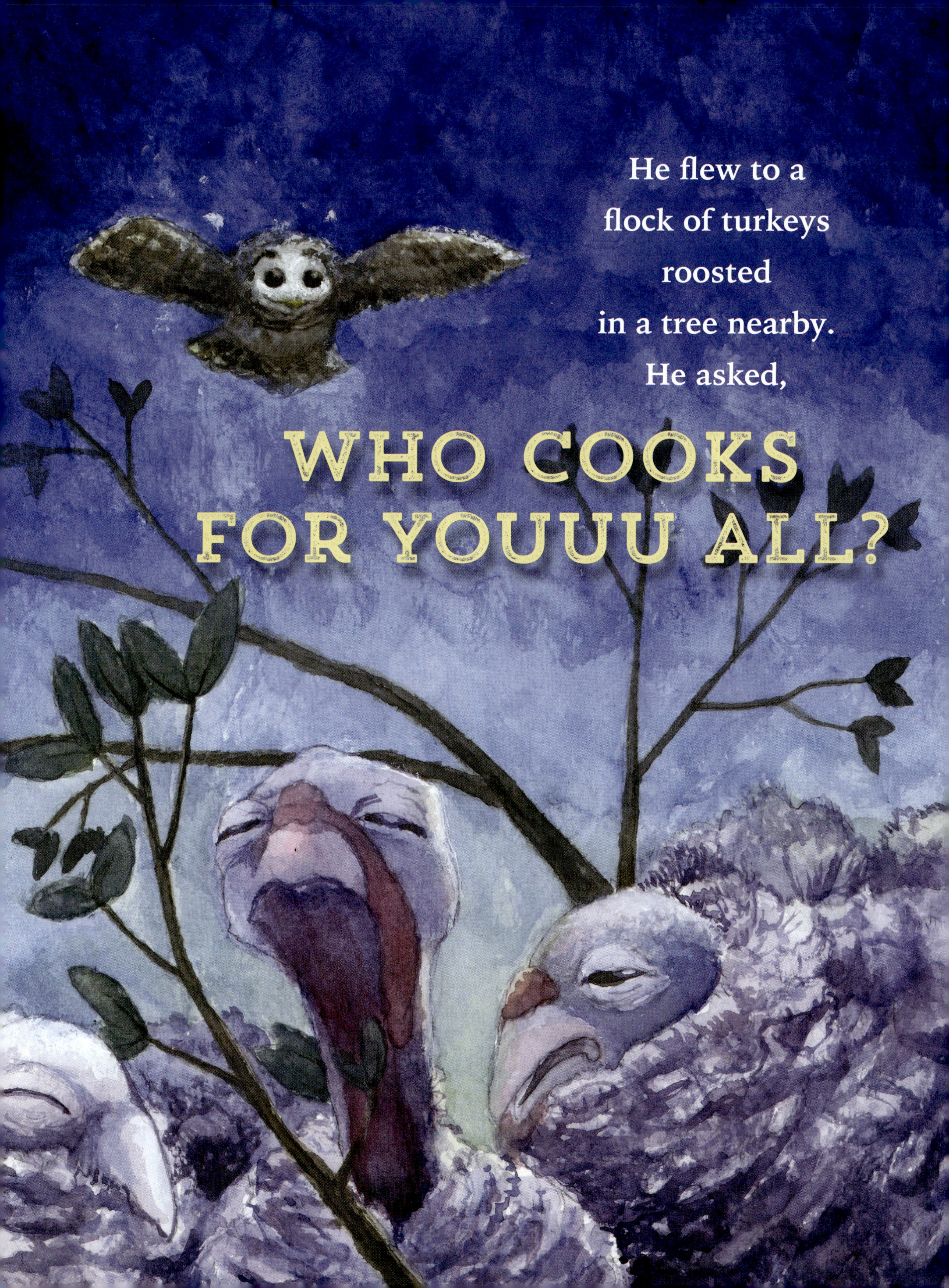
He flew to a
flock of turkeys
roosted
in a tree nearby.
He asked,
WHO COOKS
FOR YOUUU ALL?

It was chaotic.

Their gobbles meant

"Ah!"

GOBBLE,
GOBBLE,
GOBBLE!

"Yikes!"

GOBBLE,
GOBBLE,
GOBBLE!

"Eek!"

GOBBLE,
GOBBLE,
GOBBLE!

They all flapped and wobbled away—
leaving Howie alone once again.

Now Howie was running out of time. Soon the woods would be busy and bright.

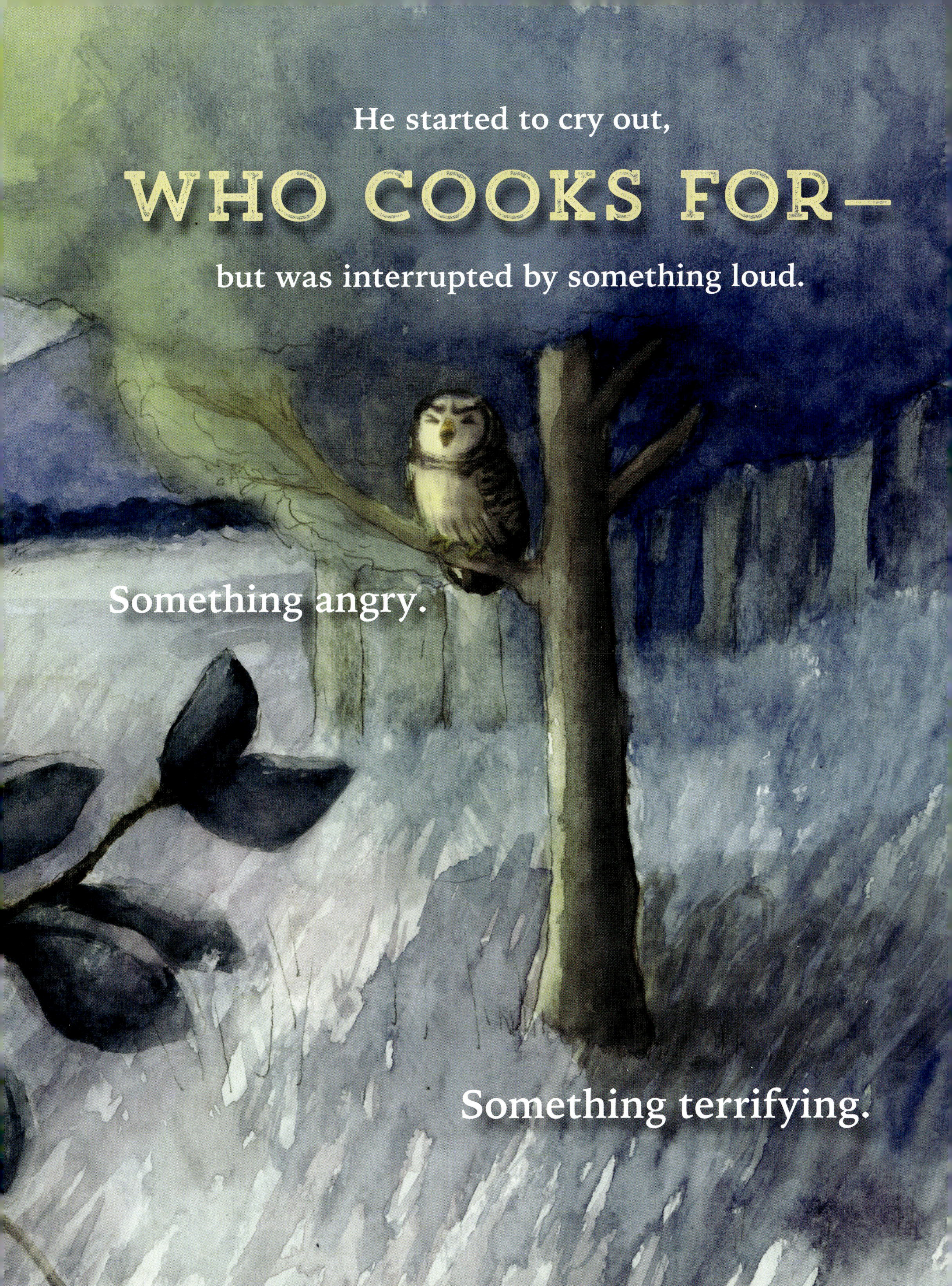

He started to cry out,

WHO COOKS FOR—

but was interrupted by something loud.

Something angry.

Something terrifying.

A small crow.

And the crow's caws meant
"Go away!"
CAW!

"Begone!"
CAW!

"Just leave!"
CAW!

So Howie quickly flew away.

The sun continued to rise.

All Howie could do was softly whisper,

WHO COOKS FOR
YOUUU?

Only this time it meant . . .

“I’m sad.”

He was so distracted by his crying sniffles,
his belly growls, and the noisy forest around him
that he almost didn't hear the ZZZIP from below.
It was a girl—and she was pointing
to where she ate breakfast.

Finally, *oh finally*, someone had answered his question!

Howie flew and flew in the direction
where she pointed.

As the last golden hues of the sunrise
turned into blue sky,

he happily sang out one last

WHO COOKS FOR YOUUU?

And *this* time, it meant . . .

OPEN

“I’m full!”

Turn the page
for some fun barred owl facts!

DID YOU KNOW?

Barred owls have excellent eyesight (much better than ours). But they can't move their eyeballs as we do, so in order to look left and right, they have to turn their whole head!

Their hearing is even better than their eyesight. Unlike humans' ears, their ears are asymmetrical, which means they sit unevenly on the owl's head. It helps them pinpoint exactly where a sound is coming from.

Many birds have smooth feathers, but owl feathers are a bit fluffier. This helps them fly very quietly, making them excellent hunters.

For more owl facts and teacher resources, visit www.KatyJoTurner.com.